I Love Gray

Making Change Happen

Richard Jozwiakowski

Bloomington, IN  Milton Keynes, UK

authorHOUSE®

AuthorHouse™
1663 Liberty Drive, Suite 200
Bloomington, IN 47403
www.authorhouse.com
Phone: 1-800-839-8640

AuthorHouse™ UK Ltd.
500 Avebury Boulevard
Central Milton Keynes, MK9 2BE
www.authorhouse.co.uk
Phone: 08001974150

First published by AuthorHouse 7/24/2006

ISBN: 1-4259-5027-2 (e)
ISBN: 1-4259-5035-3 (sc)

Library of Congress Control Number: 2006906220

Printed in the United States of America
Bloomington, Indiana

This book is printed on acid-free paper.

Table of Contents

Chapter 10: Deliver Faster and Cheaper

Subtitle: More Value Does Not Mean Cheaper, Remind Them What You Are Doing

Introduction

THIS BOOK IS the result of a commitment that I made to the many people who reported to me. I would often, during our town hall meetings, tell them that I was going to write a book called I Love Gray. Usually they would look at me quizzically and ask "What?" I would invariably respond that people are comfortable with things that are black and white- clearly defined and no doubt. I felt, and still believe, that too much comfort breeds a laissez faire attitude resulting in a company's demise. Why? Change is the only constant in today's business world. People, who are comfortable in the black and white, don't see the change coming- or who aren't living in the GRAY, will go the way of the buggy whip. I, therefore, love gray because venturing into it enables me to become more comfortable that the future will, in fact, be more secure.

Today, more information is available then ever before. According to some recent surveys, productivity has actually decreased due to the enormous amount of information available. I have turned around 4 different organizations of various sizes by subscribing to the belief that changing an organization secures its future and am compelled to share some views with you. Because of the myriad of information available, I have kept this book short to hopefully help simplify how you can sort through this information overload. I have been exposed to many organizational styles and even more managerial styles. This short book is an attempt to share, and hopefully distill what I have learned from others. As is the case with other information, there is an increasing number of "how to" managerial books. Some of the books are good and some are not. This book, while I am attempting to make it good, is directed at people on the way up the ladder. You get to the top by making mistakes, by observing others, by improving your business, and by having the proper mentors. This book is hopefully going to help you make less (visible) mistakes by providing real life examples for middle managers and is written with excerpts from 20 years of practical experience. If you find a section that is of little value to you, move on to the next chapter. I do recommend that you read chapters 1, 3, 6 and 9. Contained therein are the elements to ensure balanced performance.

My credentials: I enjoy turning around organizations needing improvement. Obviously, the more improvement needed, the easier the task. I have turned around four different organizations (Tripling revenue in a flat market and concurrently increasing margins tenfold, increasing customer satisfaction – the totally satisfied - three fold, improving employee morale and lessening turnover while getting the promotions and recognition as accomplishments became recurring).

Keeping it simple, focusing on profitable growth, customer satisfaction, employee development, and process improvement, help you achieve your objective. As simple as that sounds, what I find most astounding is how many people don't take the time to establish <u>achievable goals</u>, and they get overwhelmed by the process. God did not make the world in one day, He took a whole week. Most of us are less powerful and need to recognize that. On the other hand, if you are in a gym and vigorously spin your wheels for a long time, you produce a lot of sweat but don't usually end up in a different room. Analogies aside (for the moment), you need continuous, measurable improvement, which over time will help you attain your longer term objective. All this entails change, since the world is not standing still.

Being able to understand where you and your organization stand, and recognizing that you can make a difference, is a very powerful aphrodisiac. It makes you want to get up for work, even after a bad day, or even a bad week. And since you are spending more time at work, why not enjoy it? As many previous authors on Business Management have stated, if you are uncomfortable with your current environment, then change something. The benefits that you derive are not only self improvement, but a legacy that carries forward after you have moved on. That legacy resides in the management team that has benefited from your coaching and experience. Even after moving on, I still have former reports call periodically for advice. Just as satisfying, I see them utilizing what they have learned and carrying it to an even greater level. In reading this book, hopefully you too will find a nugget or two that will help you in this changing world. I know, because the ideas contained herein, have helped me not only turn around troubled organizations, but also befriended me with people who still call me occasionally for support, a question, or just to maintain contact. And those personal relationships are most rewarding.

Chapter 1

How Comfortable Are You Really

Creating Discomfort with the Present

LIKE MANY NEW managers, I felt that I knew what needed to be done to the organization that I inherited and was convinced that I could make those changes in less than six months and tout my success. I quickly discovered that most people within the organization that I was to manage were comfortable with the status quo. Coming in, I knew that they could do better but did not understand why they were not ready for change. I learned over time, that my main task, as their leader, was to motivate them to accomplish my objective. I needed to modify my leadership style to both drive for greater success while acknowledging accomplishments. In order to do this, one of my biggest challenges was assessing how comfortable I was with them and how comfortable was my organization.

Ask questions to understand
where comfort zones reside

When I was interviewing with one of my potential employers, the interviewers made it crystal clear- change was needed. They had had 3 people hold the position that I was interviewing for, all in a total of 18 months. Customers were telling them that they liked the product but disliked the support organization (which was my team). The interviewers made it clear that no internal management succession plan was in place, nor were any of the direct reports capable of being promoted. Was I comfortable? Surprisingly, yes. I am a change agent; management supported change, had a sense of urgency, and wanted clear action. I also was not comfortable with the state of the support organization.

I interviewed my staff as soon as I came on board. They all thought that they were doing a great job but just needed more people and more freedom. Unfortunately, they were also not making money, and everyone outside the immediate team felt that they were not meeting minimal requirements.

The need exists to create discomfort
with the current environment

My biggest challenge was to make the team uncomfortable with the current environment so they were willing to accept change. The average person in the organization had 26 years with the company, and most of them had over 10 years in their current position. Turnover was 2 – 4%, with most coming through retirement. I was a new "outsider", so what did I know. As I tried to implement change, the team was quick to point out why this particular change had failed years ago. After all, they knew that once I had another 10 years with the company, then I would know that the problem was not them but all the others. They also knew that my predecessors did not last long, so they established a pool to determine how long I would last.

To build my confidence, one manager said he had the most time - 14 months!

Use customer feedback to substantiate weaknesses

Shortly after I started, I held our first team meeting. At the meeting, I presented comments from our customers- most of which were negative. This data was taken from previous customer surveys and reflected why the management thought our customer satisfaction was low. I also interviewed other organizations, and quickly, they lined up outside my door to help me with their recommendations. The VP of sales even gave every one of the dissatisfied customers my phone number and suggested that they call me. I recognized quickly that I had to develop a strategy and communicate it to everyone. We had multiple holes in the dike, but only had a limited number of fingers to plug them with.

I knew that I had to identify the top 3-6 priorities and ensure those goals did not slip as we expanded the number of items that we were working on. Most prior failures were due to attempting to address too many issues and fixing none of them. My solutions were either too limited or not quick enough for others, or were too demanding for my existing staff. In no time, the people with the most seniority (in position, not title), used their knowledge of the organization to establish roadblocks, knowing that if I failed, they would be able to continue doing what they had done for the last 26 years. What they didn't realize is that they did not have 26 years experience, but one year experience that they repeated 26 times. They were comfortable with the status quo even if we weren't making money. That was other people's problems. I had to have a success quick!

Set the tone by personally addressing issues

I determined that initially I needed to be a hands-on manager.

I started calling our largest customers and asked them what they liked and what they didn't. Where there were communication issues, I gave them my personal phone number and told them to call me if things went awry. After all, I would rather try and fix an upset customer than have him call others and have them tell me how to fix the problem. I also had my managers share my pain. First, we needed to get the managers to own problems that they could control. Secondly, we had to offload some the actionable items to focus on the highest priorities. I knew that I could help with advice, and provide support when the manager did not know what to do. But I needed the team to change what they were doing wrong. I compiled action lists which I shared with these customers. I reviewed them with my staff and made them uncomfortable when they were not acted on. Initially, I was unpopular with my staff, but slowly started to gain some satisfied customers. The managers were seeing action and had two choices: either do something that they were uncomfortable with, or find someplace else to finish their careers. They reluctantly took on one or two actions to modify their current approach.

Reality was taking on a new form. I was now in a position to begin to alter my managerial style. If I was to be successful over the longer term, I needed to delegate, freeing myself to do some strategic planning and developing or replacing the people who were accountable for achieving our objectives. What was not clear was what our objectives were and where we were headed. My marketing background convinced me that I needed to understand our environment. My results-oriented personality and my bosses said I needed to get things fixed quickly. My logic said that I needed to prioritize or I too would go the way of my predecessors. I decided that I needed to assess where we were at quickly and then produce results.

Chapter 2

Assess the Market & Customer Views

Compare to Competition with Brutal Honesty

IT WAS EASY to fix problems like miscommunication or lack of follow-up to promised actions. Now customers were demanding more. The price was too high, they wanted compensation for previous pain, and they wanted it for years to come. I knew what I had experienced in previous markets, but this one was different. I needed to know what the competitors were doing; after all, we were losing money and yet were being told we were too high. Then why was the competition making money and yet had better customer satisfaction?

In order to understand the market, you need to understand where your company is

So, that is what I did first. I calculated revenue per employee and cost per employee. While that may sound easy, it took some time. The revenue had to be calculated on actual auditable revenue, not including pull thru revenue, potential revenue or discounts given by others that were restated on our books. The expenses had to include salaries, fringe benefits, and overtime and bonuses. Needless to say, I was surprised to find that even though we were growing revenue at double digit rates, our expenses were growing at a rate of 6% more than our revenue. We were on a fast track to bankruptcy and didn't even know it. Bonuses were being paid on both revenue and expenses. While this may sound good, they were each paid separately. Managers quickly learned that if they set a conservative expense budget, they could under-run expenses, miss revenue targets and still receive a decent bonus. I immediately created a financial based bonus for future years, which was the net of revenue minus expenses (or contribution margin). At the lower levels, we could not track all fixed expenses so we calculated the contribution margin on variable expenses. As we moved up in the organization, we added other controllable expenses as we could. This bonus element was paired with another element focused on customer satisfaction.

The net impact was increased focus on incremental change, not on the longer 80 yard run. Convincing the management team that they could improve, and not fail, was a challenge. Previously, their only benchmark was other mediocre teams. They also were accustomed to "adjustments" to their targets in mid-year when they were falling short; after all, it was the changing environment causing their shortfall, not their management actions!

Performance needs to be benchmarked versus competitors

That is where external benchmarks proved to be so overwhelming. Of course, at first, it was "a sampling", then it was "selected data". Over time however, it became fact- we weren't doing well and the competition was beating our butt!

These surveys became our bible. And if we didn't believe them, we had our administrative people call our customers to get first hand feedback. Initially, our personnel had the openly strong opinion that the customer who provided the feedback was wrong- and openly told him so! This feedback was impacting his compensation and therefore only positive comments were acceptable. Continued surveys, externally, however, proved these chastisements wrong, and over time they began to change attitudes. Close monitoring of how discussions were conducted with customers was also important. We would not have known about customers being told that they were wrong (affecting compensation), if we had not followed up personally with the customer.

Ensure that data is accurate

Any data collected initially, needed to be substantiated. It does no one any good if the data collected is skewed to support the beliefs of the person conducting the survey. I found it extremely beneficial to use a third party organization to conduct the survey. Albeit, it was more costly and required much more work upfront to ensure that the questions weren't leading, but the results were more pure. Attention to what questions to ask- what do we want to know- required considerable back and forth dialog. Fortunately, with a lot of interviewing, we found a firm that knew what they were doing and expected us to act on the results that they compiled. In the selection process, we also interviewed firms who could charge more, provide voluminous reports, but only substantiated their preconceived views. You don't want the cheapest, what you want is a firm that provides you with meaningful data that helps you measure your starting point and your progress to your goal. Working in a business to business environment, we found that our initial customer database was fraught with incorrect contacts, incorrect addresses and even non-existent customers. In working with many IT organizations and consulting firms, we have found this to be a common malady. In fact, we even had a customer who swore his data was >90% correct until we both tested the data. After some cleansing of the data, we then had to establish contact guidelines with our customers. Some liked daily or weekly contact while others preferred semi annual or annual contact. Obviously, if the customer is one of your largest accounts, you want to ensure some level of communication of facts on a fairly frequent basis and at multiple levels. Properly prepared and presented, we had one customer declare that our reports had "established a new standard for the industry". Improperly done, either due to conflicting data or erroneous contacts, we had customers challenge our data. The important point to note is that survey data is only valuable if you use it to assess your progress and continually work on improving your performance and the eventual outcome.

Greater impact occurs when data is shared internally

The data collected had high exposure within our organization. At first, the results were totally unacceptable to management. Instead of viewing this as a negative, we converted this into a positive- the data was used to sell why we needed to change. Even though it was challenged initially, continued surveys substantiated the results and aided in providing progress reports. Concurrently, by benchmarking against others, you are able to establish statistically aggressive but achievable goals. It is quite intuitive that if you have 20% market share, to assume a target of 70% market share within the next year may not be an achievable goal. The data, properly assembled, with a good survey firm, enables you to project a reasonable target to your management. As time progressed, the customer data enabled us to modify our short term goals to the areas with the most positive impact. In the course of seven years, we went from being in the bottom 20% for comparable organizations to being in the top 20%.

Most importantly, understanding where we stood enabled us to grow both revenue and profit.

The Roman Empire did not materialize overnight. It took years of planning, with the plans being changed as the situation changed, as mistakes were made, and as differing personalities became involved. So too it was with our organization. But before the foundation was in place- before a strategic plan was implemented, we had to assess both the market and where we stood. Quickly enough, I could get buried in the detail of daily activities, I had to take advantage of my new position and factually assess where we stood. With data in hand, we could then develop our plan.

Chapter 3

Set A Vision

And Resell It Over and Over

ONCE YOU HAVE assessed your organization and the market place, you are ready to move forward. You can choose to ready, shoot, aim as many managers do, or you can establish a target. As many a military commander would say, we need to make sure whom we are shooting at, for the enemy could be us. Most gurus on goal setting suggest that you establish not less than 3 nor more than 6 goals. I chose four: increased profitability, increased customer satisfaction, improved people development and improved processes.

Goals must be balanced to achieve vision

Noble as the goals were, they required fine tuning to ensure that they were measurable, achievable and enabled continuous improvement. Let's say that your market assessment shows that your revenue per person is $80,000 per year and your competitor's revenue per person is $170,000. Clearly, you would like to get to where they are- if your other primary goals are able to be achieved. If your other goals are increased customer satisfaction and increased growth in revenue, simply doubling your price is not going to help you achieve your goals. In my case, I chose to set a vision of $120,000 revenue per person. The first response to that vision was disbelief. My management team did not believe it possible. I therefore provided them with market data that demonstrated where others were and gave them a few suggestions on how they could work their way to the goal. Secondly, I gave them this vision as a 3 year goal and set a much more achievable one year target. I asked them to increase the revenue per person to $120,000 for new accounts only. This provided some relief since many did not know how to increase prices for existing customers. With new accounts only, we could match competitive pricing- which turned out to be higher, while still garnering an increase over our existing base. I also asked them to assess their expenses to ensure that every additional dollar of revenue exceeded the increased expense. They were also asked to assess how they were managing existing accounts and identify cost savings opportunities which did not negatively impact customer satisfaction.

The 20-60-20 Rule

All organizations have innovators, fence-sitters and non-believers. The split typically is 20-60-20. You want to support the top 20 while ensuring that the bottom 20 do not consume most of your time. If you get the top 20 to succeed and the middle 60 are continually shown the rewards reaped by the top 20, you will make converts out of them. On the other hand, if you let the naysayers dominate your time with excuses and rationale as to why things can't be done, you are defeated before you get out of the gate. The objective therefore is to share the vision, provide demonstrated success stories while squelching the non-believers. You will not be able to totally shut down their views because you are not with them most of the time. You can, however, set the tome in formal sessions by focusing on the positives and continually selling your vision over and over. I, personally, found it beneficial to alter, ever so slightly, the analogies, or examples or comparisons so that they were not redundant but the vision was always the same.

Using analogies, as in comparing the balance of a 3 legged stool or a four legged chair to that of a unicycle, enabled me to provide alternatives that a person can relate to as I lay out the vision. Relating back to the 3 to 6 goals mentioned earlier, can you imagine the lack of clarity in vision if you had enough goals to fill a bus? By the time the bus was full, most people would be hard pressed to state the goals, let alone achieve them. On the other hand, too few goals, or a lack of balance, make the riding the unicycle achievable, but not something sustainable over a long period of time.

Operational goals are only steps toward your vision

A vision is something in the foreseeable future, hence I prefer either a 2 or 3 year perspective. If too short, it becomes operational goals not a vision. If the vision is too far out, it is difficult to demonstrate measurable progress toward that goal. A clear vision helps you establish measurable goals that achieve incremental improvement. Continual incremental improvement helps you reach the goal that was originally established; however, by then, you have enhanced or redirected the vision as the market has evolved. Hence the vision is more a direction or ideal, which may never be achieved, but if achieved, is viewed as a panacea. In the example cited earlier, once the $120,000 goal was achieved, the vision had shifted to $170,000 – which is where the competition had been throughout. However by balancing with customer satisfaction, we were able, over time, to demonstrate better customer satisfaction than competitors while still striving for the increased revenue. Having achieved the $120,000 enabled the new vision to become a perceived achievable objective since the easier one had been accomplished. Just as importantly, it made believers out of the fence-sitters and converted them to followers. Concurrently, the non-believers either became converts or left for what they perceived as greener pastures.

Every meeting with employees started and ended with the vision, and as time progressed included success stories. I thought that I was so redundant that no one could miss the message. Surprisingly, employee surveys indicated that they still were not receiving enough communication as to the strategic direction of the organization. The lesson that I learned is that once you have developed a strategy, it needed to be repeated frequently, and when you think you are saying the same thing too often, repeat it again. To ensure that the message was fresh, I would use different analogies, or different customer references, but always keep the same summary points to deliver the message.

Chapter 4

Develop Your Team

Challenge Them To Do Better Than
They Think They Can

ONE OF THE "bibles" that I used with people that worked for me was the Leadership Pipeline by Ram Charan, Stephen Drotter and James Noel. In it they clearly differentiate the difference between an individual contributor and a manager (actually, they use the term leader). When you are an individual contributor, it is all about you and your performance. When you are a successful leader, it is all about how well you develop your team. It is hard work because firstly it requires a headset change on your part.

How much time is really
spent on people development?

I used to tell my new managers to record their time for a week and how it is spent. It does not have to be minute by minute but should identify the major time elements in at least half hour increments. How much time is spent on email, in meetings, on paperwork, etc? Once completed, calculate what percent was spent in working with your subordinates: coaching, defining work to be done, communicating (both at their request as well as yours), providing direction and measurements, as well as taking ownership for their results. You will invariably find that they have spent less than 5% in planning and people development. A good manager should attempt to spend at least 20% of his time in this new area.

Most people want to do a good job. Most bring a set of skills, but are lacking in some areas. All are different and that enables you to build a team. You want to find the best people and develop your management team as businessmen (or women). I used to tell each of the 30+ managers in our $100M business that they each ran their own $3M business. Since that size business was as large as 90% of the businesses in the US, they needed to figure out how to think like an entrepreneur and grow their business. Most managers in larger organizations come in thinking that if they managed their costs and minimized turnover, they were managing their business. I believe that if you don't attempt to grow your business and make changes, eventually your business will go the way of the buggy whip.

Constructive feedback must be positive and include examples on how to succeed.

Jack Welch believed that "success will come from the reflected glory of your team, not what you do". Jack did have some success at GE. In mentoring people, you need to exude confidence about the future and demonstrate that you care about their success. You need to challenge them to do their best. I am continually amazed by how many managers fail because they did not clearly set aggressive, achievable goals. The goals must be clear and measurable so that you, as a leader, can monitor their progress and provide feedback throughout the year. With new managers, I liked to have daily meetings initially to ensure that they understood what my goals were and how they could help me achieve them. I then started communication with them weekly as they set their own priorities. At this point, it helps to challenge them to do their best (usually better than they think they can do). This is where the positive vision comes into play. You are providing feedback, and, if you're honest, you are addressing both their strengths and their weaknesses. Whether they have just made a presentation or a customer visit, they need to know what resonated well and what needs work. Constructive feedback must be constructive. Most people, me included, do not receive criticism well. In fact many people, even if given 90% positive feedback, will dwell on the other 10% if you let them. This is where the real coaching comes into play. If you help them understand how to correct that 10%, and let them practice what they are taught, most will succeed. Managers are also motivated by receiving recognition for their accomplishments. If you focus solely on their need for improvement, they get discouraged and give up. Over time, I modified my managerial style to the individual. While some people can take the input and move on, finding that balance between praise and coaching is unique to each individual. That is why it is so important to work closely with your team. Many new managers and some seasoned managers want to take over when the new manager is failing. This undermines all the positive coaching. You need to be there to help shore them up if they fail, but you need to allow increasing freedom as they venture out. The key is keeping the end objective in mind. I am continually surprised at how great some of the ideas and plans are from my subordinates as they develop and spread their wings. There is a fine balance between candor and criticism. You have to honest, but that always needs to be followed up with how the negative can be converted to a positive. If you stick to your values while exuding a positive vision, it will be accepted.

Personal development can be
better motivation than pay raises

One manager, whom I knew earlier in my career, was reluctant to develop his people. He was afraid that he would spend all his time developing people to only have them leave for greener pastures or, worse yet, take his job! I have found that I want managers to take my job- how else will I get promoted if I don't have someone ready to take over? I also want my job to be easier; I'd rather have them do it right than have to do it myself. If you want an example of success, just look at the people that were developed at GE and are now successful in their own right as CEO's of other large organizations. Your people don't have to strive for the CEO position, but they do need to be coached to strive for continued personal development and ongoing success. I also have found increasing loyalty from people that I have developed. As long as you show that you really care about their personal development, they will stay. One year, during a lengthy performance review, we began discussing developmental goals for the coming year. At that point, my report looked at me and said that he had been offered a job elsewhere with a 20% raise. He went on to say that he refused the job because he felt that a better job would be available in the future if he stayed and continued his personal development. He believed that his personal development would be more likely in his current environment and that would result in even better opportunities in the future. I am not naïve enough to think that all people will act that way, but a positive developmental environment will enable people to think clearly and not look for the next green pasture. I also want some of my team to be promoted. After all, what better reflection of your managerial skills is having a disciple carry forward some of your concepts to another organization.

Training takes many forms and I believe in utilizing them all. Nowadays, a common view is that managers need to be college-degreed. Conceptually, I agree with the thought, since having completed a college curriculum teaches people certain disciplines that are required in management. I, however, prefer the concept of college degree *or equivalent.* This enables you to choose the best person and not just evaluate based on who has the best sheepskin. Also needed, though, are formal managerial courses. During my career, I found that certain marketing courses helped develop my strategic thinking, while certain managerial courses helped me understand how to develop others and get the best out of them. I did discover, though, that some of my reports preferred direct situational coaching. Many times, formal training resonates, but then the theory is difficult to apply when you return to your work environment. Real time situational coaching enables the person being taught to question, evaluate and adjust real time. Formal learning on the other hand, enables you to reflect on the lesson, while not having the pressure of a real life situation. In my opinion, a balance of these creates a lifetime of learning.

One facet of learning is continual reinforcement

We all have a fragile psyche, and that is why refresher courses and reminders on the end goals are so important. A well trained confident team will know when they are good. They will be able to compare themselves to others and know that they are both strategic thinkers and true businessmen. This does require daily effort on your part. Over time, the more you spend on training and coaching, the time you will spend firefighting will diminish. This will free you for more strategic planning and market assessment. This gets back to understanding each individual, their needs and their drivers. Regardless of your business size, you cannot do everything. You are dependent on others. Understanding that requires you to develop your team and choose each new hire carefully. Regardless of the training approach that you utilize, you need people who have the desire to improve. You can always teach people about product specific or company specific features and benefits. You cannot teach desire. All you can do is lay the foundation for success; their performance is what will determine their individual accomplishments. You, as their coach, choose the people to help you be successful and help guide them to blossom. Seeing that happen is indeed rewarding.

Chapter 5

Be Prepared for Subversive Efforts

FACTS AND MEASUREMENTS are essential for your success. Enough people have been burnt by being too trusting, therefore it essential that you hold true to your vision and establish measures to monitor success. Time will eventually show that you mean what you say, but at the beginning, you need to take smaller steps to begin to establish credibility before the naysayers undermine you.

Beware of the status quo

Many people accept the status quo. This does not mean that they like it; it means that they fear the unknown. Within this fear, is a desire to accept that which is known. When you set a vision which requires change, resistance will appear because the suspicion is that things will get worse. In each of the organizations that I was brought into, one overwhelming statistic was common. Most people had worked in the organization for a long time. In the first several, the average tenure was in excess of 26 years. In the latest one, the average tenure was seven years, with the "founding fathers" having in excess of 12 years.

Therefore, in all, they had developed a daily routine and felt like they were successfully contributing. After all, were they not receiving a monthly paycheck and annual pay raises? In most cases, performance reviews, if given, only said positive things about them.

I'll digress for just a moment to state that I have always been viewed as a fair, but demanding manager. Simply stated, once goals were established, I expected them to be met. What I have found is that weak managers either set unclear goals and measurements, or they adjust the goals as circumstances (viewed as beyond control) change. This often results in people spending as much time rationalizing their actions regardless of the outcome. When running a business, even if you are a first line manager in a large organization, you need to be successful for your organization to avoid decay and demise. Numerous examples can be cited from the transportation industry (trains) to the steel industry to the auto industry to the airline industry, where people were continually rewarded, while new competitors arose and eventually took away market share and eventually jobs were lost. In order to avoid the eventual decline, change must be embraced, as long as it has a clearly defined outcome that positions you for the near future.

Expect progress and make sure that it can be measured

I followed the steps that I outlined in the previous chapters, but often had push back before measurable results were achieved. It is therefore essential to assume this will happen and be prepared for it. The people who were around for a long time had developed an informal network to achieve what they thought would be best for them. The non-believers use this informal network to set up incorrect assumptions of the outcome and to build fear of what is to come. There are several ways to address this, but you do not want to be all consumed by these naysayers. What you need to do is develop a method of gathering facts that support your vision and which provide stepping stones for your journey. Logical arguments will be presented that infer that the path that you are on will lead to failure of others. Your facts need to support your vision. You cannot directly attack relationships that have been built over 5, 10, or 20 years. That is why the facts have to be related to the actions taken, not focused on those content with the status quo. As mentioned in chapter 2, if you have properly assessed the market and customer views, the facts will come from subsequent follow-up with them as well. Initially, it is with one customer, or one market segment, but as time progresses, that builds to more customers and more market segments supporting your facts. In addition to that, you have a set of internal numbers- revenue per person, expenses on a year to year comparison, or whatever parameters are pertinent- that substantiate that the vision has merit and that others will benefit from your teams success.

One of the easiest areas to gain support is within the sales organization. Sales people are paid on commission, if you help them achieve greater commissions, they will quickly align with you. Here too, you have to be careful to help the sales people who have good business sense, not just those few who will sell at any price to get the sale. Fortunately, I have worked in businesses that require ongoing relationships. This, for the most part, requires good businessmen in sales, since their *next* commission is based on how satisfied the customer is with the present deal. This helps provide a balanced exchange, since, if the company does not make money, it will not be able to honor the terms to the full satisfaction of the customer. Remember, most people want to do a good job, most want to do what is right. Invariably, everyone will bring up extreme examples to support their position. That is why it is important to have the early victories defined by the facts that you seek to accomplish your vision.

<u>Publicize the successes</u>

The successes help sell your vision, they must therefore be touted. When building a new structure, the foundation must be solid, or the structure will collapse as it increases in size. Your facts must therefore be irrefutable and known to all. Some may look at this as too much braggadocio, therefore it must be properly couched. One battle won does not end the war. You will be more successful if you emphasize how this success is but a step towards future successes which are in line with the vision which you have espoused. You therefore should work with the innovators, the leaders who add credence to the positive steps to the end goal. I still have personal relationships with people that have been highly successful in sales that initially challenged and then worked with me toward a mutually successful goal.

I mentioned in Chapter 3 that you should not let the 20% that are negative on your vision dominate your time. This does not mean that you should totally ignore them either. They have, in some instances, succeeded by undermining others that they did not agree with. They can also do that to you. You need to quickly identify who they may be and thwart their efforts. Challenging them head on can give them the credence that they need to continue. On the other hand, focusing on facts which support your vision will demonstrate that their views are unfounded. An example might help clarify this point.

<u>Progress must be balanced</u>
<u>to achieve long term success</u>

Some people believe that customer satisfaction is paramount, even if it means sacrificing profit. Some even carry it to the extreme that increasing pricing will undermine customer satisfaction. I am a strong advocate of customer satisfaction; it is one of my four primary points of focus. It must however be balanced with the other three- financial improvement, people development and process improvement. We had a customer who had a reputation as being very difficult to satisfy. Both the sales rep and the service rep believed that since this customer gave us lots of business that was only possible to continue if we did everything that this customer wanted. I met with this customer and he spent almost two hours telling me everything that we did wrong. After listening to this diatribe, I asked him why he still did business with us. He replied that we, unlike our competition, always did what we committed to. After the meeting, I worked with the sales and service reps and we jointly developed what we would do and what the customer needed to do so we both could be successful. We then scheduled another meeting with the customer to present our action plan. We needed the customer's acceptance of this plan to continue. Once we achieved this, we worked on our actions and reviewed these periodically with him. Over time, we completed our items, but the customer did not complete what he had agreed to. He began demanding that we do his tasks for him at no additional cost to him. I reviewed the original action plan with him and pointed out that he had not completed the actions that he had agreed to, and that we would do his items as well for additional cost. By having the original agreement, adhering to it, and periodic progress reviews, we were able to curb the continual increase in demands. This built credibility not only with the customer but also built credibility internally that we could increase customer satisfaction and increase profit. It required facts, documentation and action. It also demonstrated to others what could be done without directly confronting those who were resisting the change needed. This one account helped lessen potentially subversive efforts at other accounts, thus expediting the changes needed.

Chapter 6

Auditing Progress

Follow up, But Don't Break the Weak

IT IS ALWAYS a balance between following up on individuals yet not micromanaging to the point of breaking the weak. There are multiple ways to audit the progress. Several alternatives are listed below:

Ask employees 2 levels down questions

You have your direct reports repeating your strategy and vision in meetings and other team forums, yet you don't see the results. That may be OK, but you need to find out if your team is on track. You can grill your report and second guess every step along the way or you can spend time with their reports. Obviously, being the boss of their boss, the employees are going to be quite guarded when you first meet with them. One approach that I used with a multiple location team, incorporated team meetings or what we termed town hall meetings. The first objective was to get the time to deliver my state of the business, our strategy for the short term and to get employee feedback. The first phase included a one hour presentation which not only told them what I hoped to accomplish but also provided updates on the state of the company and, to a lesser extent, what the company wanted to accomplish. Always an attention getter was what is in it for them. Whether it was potential for promotions, additional training, status on benefits, or squelching rumored layoffs, I always was blunt and did not give what some employees referred to as "corporate smoke and mirrors". I always kept in mind that these were adults who were key players in our future and concerned about a more secure future. The second part included another guest speaker- either local sales manager who presented recognition for specific individuals or someone from another department to talk about how their needs tied to our objectives. The third part was supposed to be the gist of the meeting, wherein any employee could ask any question or render any opinion. I had just one rule- it had to be professionally presented and could not attack a specific individual personally. It could however be constructive input as to how to make their environment or the company better. I also took good notes in this section to make sure that all issues were followed up on and reported back to them if the issue was not resolved in the meeting. Depending on the attendees, there usually was one individual who had a reputation for always speaking out. As long as they did not ramble on and on, I always let them speak out and responded where appropriate. Sometimes if I knew that the group would be reticent, I would, before the meeting, ask one of the team to bring up a particular concern of his in the Q&A session. Over time, however, I found out that the fourth part of the meeting was where information was really gathered. Since these sessions were infrequent, particularly when managing a nation-wide group, that a reception after the meeting was beneficial and appreciated. We had several ground rules: The employees were reminded that since this was considered a company function that they had to maintain corporate decorum even if they were drinking. If they were returning to work, or had a long trip home, they were encouraged not to consume alcoholic beverages. Being the senior employee, I always picked up the tab. In so doing, I usually kept these sessions to an hour or so in duration. But I did mix with those in attendance and found them more willing to discuss the company, the vision and many other things in more of a one on one environment. During these sessions, I found out whether they were clearly being communicated the vision and being helped to achieve it, or whether their boss just mouthed the vision but did things his way. Sometimes, I also received some very thoughtful suggestions which would make it easier to achieve our vision if we acted on the advice. I tried very hard to make these sessions personable, but never to personal. Over time, not only did I look forward to these sessions but so did most of the team. They received insight as to why we were pursuing the vision, where we stood in the progress toward our goal, and just as importantly saw the benefits that they derived as we progressed to our objectives.

Conduct weekly staff meetings to assess teamwork and progress

As you first set the vision, you cannot assume that it is clearly understood. Even more so, you can't assume that all your team agrees with it. In one of the turnarounds, where most players were based in the same facility, we had weekly "updates". The concept was initiated by my predecessor, therefore I continued these sessions after assuming responsibility for the group. I quickly found several things wrong in my first meeting. Several of the group liked to dominate the session and rambled on and on. Others believed that this was the forum to point out to others how they were impeding progress toward our mutual goals. While all were well intended, or at least I worked on that premise, we completed the first session in 3 and half hours with little learned or accomplished. I quickly laid out some basic ground rules for our next session. Each direct report was to restrict his update to 10 to 15 minutes. Where points of contention were raised, it had to have been previously discussed with the individual involved prior to the meeting. I encouraged the individuals involved to meet one on one and not in front of an audience of their subordinates. I also required them to not disparage other managers with their reports. At one point, it got to the level that I forbid them to send more than 2 emails back and forth on the same topic. They were required to then arbitrate face to face. I even went so far as to announce this requirement at an employee town hall. Not surprisingly, the employees cheered when they heard this. One employee did push the issue by asking whether this meant that I was discouraging the use of email. I responded that we should use email for communication, particularly to document progress. I did clearly discourage the use of email as a means to raise issues with a peer, particularly without having discussed them previously. Email can also be used as a means to avoid conflict resolution. People hide behind the impersonal email so that they are not forced to discuss and make the hard decision to resolve. By following the 2 email rule, emotions are kept under control. Not surprisingly, subsequent meetings were shorter and more productive. These sessions also provided a forum for each person to present ideas that were successfully implemented. Over time, managers compared the performance of their group to others and adopted a few of the more successful ideas. Maintaining the fine line between comparing to improve overall versus comparing to disparage others was difficult at first, but became easier as they recognized they were really on the same team with supporting objectives.

Discuss individual performance plans and progress to yearend goals

Individual performance plans are intended to provide a means of measuring progress toward an agreed upon goal and to aide in decision making. Properly set and discussed prior to becoming "official", performance plans help you keep your team on the vision. Normally, these plans can be very helpful. Improperly utilized, they become a club and diminish morale. Justin Menkes in his Executive Intelligence: What All Great Leaders Have, points out that superior reasoning and problem-solving skills enable an executive to create a solution tailored to suit each situation at hand. Clearly delineated goals enable the executive to work toward that end. Your job, as a coach is to help individuals by clarifying that goal that they may be struggling with. You also can motivate someone by simply acknowledging their progress toward that goal. Key in all of this is to remind yourself about how many daily issues can detract from that goal. After all, you are running a business and every business has thousands of issues arise on daily basis. While you may not feel that you have the time to discuss progress towards these longer term goals, it is essential that you make the time to do so. You also need to be cognizant of the impact of your feedback. As mentioned earlier, you don't want to break the weak, it is vital that the feedback be constructive. What you really want is the opportunity to help that individual keep on track (or even get back on track), to the goals previously established. This is where the real coaching occurs. Proper focus on achieving the objectives, with alternatives as to how to achieve them, is what these sessions are all about. You need for your reports to make decisions by themselves; your objective is to help them with their reasoning and problem-solving, not to deride them where they make mistakes. The mistakes should be a learning vehicle, and your job is to make sure that they do not reoccur. Once they have solved their own problem, you are free to help others. You are, in effect, the teacher and benefit most when you do not solve the problem in its entirety. The more an individual grows, the more that individual (and you) benefit!

An additional benefit of these frequent sessions is that managers learn over time where they are not meeting the goals. Most are able to adjust. Those that are not develop a clear understanding of where they are falling short and may decide to seek a job that is more compatible with their abilities. I have had to help many managers find a job better suited to their skill set. I did not have to fire or layoff people because they usually made the decision on their own. The only people that I dismissed were people who violated corporate or ethics rules. In those few cases, the rest of team anticipated the action because of the frequent reviews.

Ask your customers about key issues

Your customers will always help you measure progress-if you have clearly communicated to them what your end goal is. If you haven't told your customers what your intentions are, they will fill the void. I can recall numerous meetings wherein a customer recited a litany of concerns that were not met. When debriefing with the manager involved, I would ask the simple question "Have you shared with your customer what your intentions are?" Invariably, if you don't, your customer will establish goals for you, on his own, to fill that void. Most individuals understand that you can't do everything at once and will accept progress as long as continuous improvement is noted and the end goal is understood. Too many managers today pride themselves in being fire-fighters. While dousing a house fire is essential to avoid further destruction, it does little to help you complete rebuilding the house. Comparably, your growth and your businesses growth necessitate communicating the end objective so you do not spend all your time responding to crisis resulting from a lack of communication. You can expect that your customer will remind you of something that negatively impacted him years ago. You can only control what happens in the future and the best way to do that is by agreeing what needs to be done, and then accepting the input as to the progress toward that objective. Even if the input is negative, you are in a position to rectify the problem. I would rather have negative feedback from a customer than await the inevitable dismissal emanating from a lack of communication. Positive feedback also helps motivate you to continue on your journey and achieve your objective.

Accomplishment is nothing more than achieving many small victories. Multiple books have been written on continuous improvement, six sigma, process management, etc. The objective of this chapter is to emphasize that no matter which program you utilize, the key is measured progress. Auditing that progress, by whatever means, enables you to keep the focus, and avoid much wasted time correcting (or re-doing) misguided fire-fighting.

Chapter 7

Don't Bruise the Boss's Ego

He May Be More Insecure Than You Think

MANY OF US have made the erroneous assumption that the boss has all the answers. Once we are put in that position, we realize that multiple demands and limited time require continual trade-offs. While you may spend considerable time assessing what you need to do to achieve "success", how much time have you spent assessing how to ensure that your boss is successful? Just as you have numerous demands for your time and effort, similarly, your boss has demands of him. While you have been told that you need to improve revenue by x percent, improve profitability by y, and increase market share by z, your boss may have been told that if he doesn't make customer A happy, he may lose his job. For obvious reasons you may need to understand this. Your future, and his, may not be too secure if you provide a solution to one of your problems, but, in the process tell the boss that he should have seen the problem coming. All of us achieve a certain level of success by reasoning and decision making. It is this capability that helps differentiate us. Conversely, none of us have all the answers, and in many cases, there are multiple correct solutions. As stated in the previous chapter, when assuming the role as a teacher, the key is to provide multiple options to achieving the objective, so that the individual can choose a solution that works for them. Sometimes, you may come with an even better alternative that solves the problem at hand. That does not make your boss a bad boss because he did not provide that specific solution for you. As stated in Chapter 4, once people are developed as businessmen, it is sometimes better to set them free. Your boss, if he is good leader, may in fact be doing the same thing with you.

Are you aware of the political environment?

Another factor that you need to consider is the political environment. We are a competitive lot. Wars have developed over bruised egos. Clearly, you don't want that in your workplace. You do need to understand what your boss wants to accomplish, but also, what are his career and personal objectives. In most cases, particularly the personal objectives won't be shared with you. You may need to figure them out. It is not necessary to always understand them, but it does help if you have some insight as to why your boss does what he does. In its worst form, the political environment stymies action. At its best, the environment enables success and correlated promotions. Fear will more likely prompt inaction. Praise will more likely prompt additional action. Your boss will respond in a similar fashion. A bigger bonus, a promotion, or simply praise can motivate. If you understand which the key driver of the moment is, you will help your boss be successful. Understanding the political environment helps avoid, or at least understand, sub-optimal decisions. There are times when a sub-optimal decision (or even a lost battle) enables long term success. In this context, it would be easier to accept the path chosen. Not having understood that trade-off, could result in you bruising the boss.

Most of us have worked for good bosses and not-so-good bosses. Hopefully we learn from them, enabling us to perform better under similar circumstances. In either case, understanding his drivers and his political environment, help you avoid both frustrating and embarrassing moments. At this point, I need to emphasize that I am not condoning immoral or unethical behavior. Regardless of the circumstances, you *always* need to adhere to what is right. I will, however, differentiate that from sub-optimizing. Pyrrhus, a king who defeated the Romans in 279 BC, incurred significant losses in the battle, making him too weak to fight future battles and resulted in him losing the war. In turn, you do not want to experience a Pyrrhic victory. Comparably, the more that you understand your boss's environment, the better positioned you are to ensure that both of you are successful.

Are you supporting your boss in public forums?

Early in my career, I worked with a manager who misrepresented some facts. Much to his chagrin, I challenged him and eventually uncovered the truth. Unfortunate for me, that manager was appointed as my boss about a year later. Understanding the political environment, I found employment elsewhere, before I was forced out. I did not question any of the consequences, but recognized that had I remained, I would have been worse off.

Years later, in a different organization, I encountered a similar situation. This time, understanding the political environment, I went to my boss and laid out the problem, clearly knowing that again, I could not walk away. My boss was able to address the problem in a different fashion, saving both him and me from incurring a Pyrrhic victory. You could easily say that I avoided the problem. I would counter that the issue was resolved more amiably because I understood the environment and prevented placing my boss in an untenable situation because I was aware of the potential impact that my actions would have on him. How you respond to any situation is impacted by how your boss is positioned politically. I am a change agent, and as such, have been brought into different environments to effect change. If my boss understands that change is needed and has the support of his boss that we must do things differently, support is there when dramatic change occurs. If, on the other hand, my boss wants change, but if his boss, or his peers, doesn't see the need for dramatic change, the change must be more subtle or more gradual. In either case, change is required, but how I approached it differs because the impact that it could have on both him and me. Just as I needed his support to be successful, he needed my support to achieve his objective. In the second case, others perceived some benefit was being accrued by them with the status quo. Impacting it directly would have destabilized my boss's environment. Unless he was clearly in a strong position, I could have undermined him and his ability to work with others.

A key element here is that while we often spend considerable time assessing the competitive environment, we often spend minimal time assessing the political environment. In order to achieve success, you need to ensure that your boss is successful as well. Placing him in an untenable situation only further weakens your success as well. Remember, we all have an ego. Some are more readily visible than others. If you bruise your bosses ego, you risk incurring wrath, or at the least, some uncomfortable moments in the future!

Chapter 8

Make Money

That Is Why You Are In Business

I HAVE ALWAYS been amazed at how many so called managers think that they are doing a great job, but don't really know if they are making money. We join an organization either because it is a good organization which makes money or because we've been convinced that the organization will be making money in the future. One reason that smaller or less stable companies pay more is that since there is a greater risk that they will go out of business, they feel the need to pay more to attract good talent. Occasionally, someone may join an organization at a lower than average salary because they believe that stock options will compensate them in the future to offset this lower start. While the occasional Bill Gates or William Dell will come along, greater than 90% of all start-ups fail. With that failure, significant layoffs or dismissals occur. Understanding all that, doesn't it make sense to know how your organization is doing?

<u>Understand your financials better than anyone else</u>

I briefly touched on profitability in Chapter 2 when I mentioned setting a vision. What needs to be elaborated on is how important making money is as a part of that vision. When joining a new team, one of the first things that you should do is look at the financials. At first blush, they can be quite intimidating, particularly since there is usually someone in the organization who will profess to know them inside and out. I have found that there is an inverse proportion those that loudly claim they know the numbers to how little they really know. When I was brought in to initiate a turnaround, my bosses knew we were not making money but they did not know why. My first step was to interview my direct reports and get their input. One particular individual stood out because of his self-professed knowledge of the financials. I requested that he provide a presentation comparing the previous year's performance to budget. During the presentation, I was amazed on how he could draw together what I perceived to be totally unrelated facts to support his opinion of where we were financially and why we were not on budget. He had me convinced that were doing all the correct things, but that we weren't getting credit for our efforts. His arguments were so convincing that I finally understood that he was using unrelated facts to justify his expense overruns. As we dissected the numbers, we found that we were growing revenue at 14% annually, but were growing expenses at 20%. The rationale presented included the supposition that next year we would be able to cut expenses once our startup costs associated with the growth were stabilized. Unfortunately, this rationale had been presented for two consecutive years and was included in the following year's budget submission. At the projected growth rate, we would have better off walking away from the business than continuing on the current path. Since this alternative was unacceptable, we did the next best thing- we began to segment the budget and tie factual data to each element.

I was amazed to find out that no one had been able to tie the detail of our accounts individual revenue projections with our total revenue. Years later, I was informed by a consultant that most companies assume that their database correlates to their financials, but that in most cases, the database has 60 to 70% accuracy. In our case, I broke the data down to each individual rep, holding each accountable for the accuracy of the data. Where I encountered resistance to collecting and providing the data, I informed the rep in as tactful a fashion as I could, that unless he could provide me with facts regarding his accounts, I could not afford to keep him employed. The occasional rep would find innumerable excuses as to why he did not have the time to collect the data. When all else failed, I assigned another rep to cover his accounts until the data was collected. After improving the accuracy to greater than 90%, I decided to focus on expenses. The first step is the easiest: simply take your total actual expenses and divide that by the total number of personnel. This makes it easy to compare expense per employee to revenue per employee. In our case, I found that while we were barely making money, we were increasing expenses at a faster rate than we were increasing revenue.

Understand your competitors' financials

One early and obvious step was to increase our pricing on new contracts. Of course, the initial response from both sales and customers alike were that we were not being competitive. That is where market data became a very effective tool. While the perception was that our competitors were selling for less, we found that they were packaging their offering differently. Initial quotes were lower, but when all the options requested were added in, their overall pricing was 20% higher.

This may appear to be a long winded tangent, but the point of the real life example is that you need to bury yourself in your financials until you understand them better than others. After all, have you ever had a budget presentation go well if your boss asked a question on the numbers that you were unable to provide a quick answer to? Once you understand your numbers, you need to help your reports understand them as well. In one of my turnarounds, I had 24 managers. I had each of them do semi-annual presentations. Each presentation included revenue with correlated accounts, expenses associated with major accounts and estimated margin per account. Particular focus was on new business forecasts with revenue, expense and margin projections for these new accounts. I also looked for continuous incremental improvement in margins for existing business. One of the biggest mistakes that you can make once you understand your numbers is to immediately expect a change to match the market financial leader. A better tack is to set the vision to get there and do so in small increments. I have found that small, yet aggressive goals help you enjoy occasional success. This provides motivational fuel for future improvements. The more frequent the success, the sooner that you can help your team realize that they too benefit from these successes.

Understanding the numbers in their entirety enables you to identify where you should increase expenses to fuel future growth. If you don't fully understand your financials, you will either solely focus on reducing expenses overall or invest in expensive increases that do not ever have a payback. By focusing on just reducing expenses, you eventually reach a point where the only margin improvement is by reducing personnel. While in some cases this may be justified, in most situations, it only results in reduced morale, decreased flexibility and customer dissatisfaction.

Spend is not a dirty word

On the other hand, understanding the financials let you surprise your reports by allowing large investments where the payback is evident. In the turnaround that I mentioned above, I was able, over time, to increase my number of managers from 24 to 32. I knew what the management ratio needed to be to grow the business properly and encouraged my team to add people where future growth was evident. Adding expense is not a bad thing IF you know how it will be covered. By increasing the number of managers as new opportunities were identified, and hiring new personnel before the contracts were signed we were able to actually improve margins. Previously, we had waited until the contracts were signed, incurring significant overtime expense for handling that growth, and incurring customer wrath when we did not meet all their expectations. In hiring more managers, we enabled more upfront planning and hiring to be done so the growth, when it occurred, was handled smoothly. Not only were our costs controlled, but the increased customer satisfaction generated even more revenue. This also enabled existing managers to focus on existing accounts and incremental improvements. Over an eight year period, we were able to triple revenue and increase margins by tenfold. You are in business to make money and should never forget it. As a carpenter that I hired once told me, "I am going to make money. Either I use my experience to provide a quality product (and make money), or I use my experience to make money and meet your price". Understanding the logic of that statement has always directed me to decide on making money and exceeding expectations rather than making the two mutually exclusive.

Making money is a noble goal. To do so, requires knowledge of the facts, i.e., know your financials inside and out. You should also assess how much your team knows about these facts, and share financial accomplishments with them. This will enable you to have successful budget reviews with your superiors because you will be able to demonstrate where future improvement can be made. The old cliché that 'Money breeds more money" clearly applies here because you know where your money comes from and where it will go. This enables you spend on future growth and curb spending only where it makes sense.

Chapter 9

__Communication and Agility__

Assess What Went Right,
What Went Wrong, But Stay On Strategy

HOW OFTEN HAD you heard about a manager who practiced the "Ready, shoot, aim" approach. Successful leaders establish a plan, communicate it, attempt to implement it, and continually tweak it based on what they learn as they implement. Skip any of these steps and you will most likely fall significantly short of your goal. When you do establish your plan or vision, you complete considerable analysis of what needs to be done, what can go wrong, and how to avoid it. Yet, many develop a sound plan, place it on the shelf until next year's planning session, and quickly get lost in the day to day firefighting. Having a solid plan is an excellent foundation if it is communicated to your team and you gain some level of acceptance. The reality is that no matter how solid the plan, you can't anticipate every scenario, nor provide details as to how to avoid the pitfalls which will, and do, occur. Implementing the plan can be difficult for a myriad of reasons: "how do I get started", "what if I make mistakes", "what if new situations arise" etc.

It takes real effort, and even more courage, to implement the plan. Fundamentally, you need to keep the end in site and never lose that focus.

Progress does not mean always charging ahead

Soccer players are taught at an early age that sometimes it is better to go sideways, or even backwards, to eventually move forward to the goal. Unlike American football, where every play is directed at moving to the goal, in soccer, plays are developed incorporating moving in all directions. The end goal is the same, but the strategy is different. Many leaders could learn from this sport. Much time is spent planning the approach, however the plans need to be communicated and practiced over and over. As the ability to execute improves, adjustments are made to the plans and even greater improvements are made. Sometimes an adjustment is made and turns out to be less than successful. In those cases, either the manager, or the player must display the agility to react as the real life situation occurs. In real life business situations, the leaders-whether they be managers or players- must also demonstrate that agility. Just like in soccer, too much freedom to an effective individual can result in some success for the individual but can cause the team to fall short of its goal. Tying together planning, practice, communication and agility are essential for successful organizations.

One of the most difficult parts of this process is assessing what went right and what went wrong. Here true teamwork and communication need to be displayed. A fine balance must be held between allowing the freedom to speak and ensuring that the communication is positive. No one benefits from personal attacks, while all benefit from constructive criticism. I have been told more than once that I tend to be a bit of a perfectionist. This has required me to really accepting that everyone, including me, perform at different levels. Adjusting to this has required considerable practice and a few bruised egos along the way. Achieving that goal is a tremendous feeling as long as it is not the Pyrrhic victory. You cannot lose the support of the team. This has resulted in occasional apologies, with a clear communication that achieving the goal was the objective, not attacking an individual.

To make change happen, you may need to change

The primary advantage of making change occur is that you are venturing down a new path. You can make small mistakes, readjust to get back on target and the mistakes don't continually come back to haunt you. No matter what activity you are involved in, keeping the overall goal in focus and correcting the mistake before it becomes a major problem. In the early days of a turn-around, mistakes can actually work to your benefit. How you handle the recovery is the element that can make or break you. Any good manager knows that mistakes will occur. If you take corrective action to not only resolve the issue but also to insure it does not occur again, then you have benefited from it. If, on the other hand, you try to hide the mistake or blame someone else, then you have, in effect, committed two mistakes. In dialog with my customers, I ask them what we did wrong and what would help us do better. First of all, they appreciate that you are seeking their input, making them a partner in the process. Secondly and probably more importantly, if you don't know that you have a problem, you could end up losing that customer and never know why. Many customer satisfaction publications are rife with statistics that point out how many silent customers you lose for each one that renders dissatisfaction. That is primarily why I ask for problems. If you solve it, your organization looks good, if you don't know the problem exists, you could end up with fewer customers.

Share your goals with your customers

A new customer, since he is new, has no track record of your company's performance. Sure, he chose your organization for a number of good reasons, but how often has he experienced a let down with others in the past. It is therefore essential that you communicate regularly with them. Everyone with frequent customer contact will tell you that they communicate with the customer. What is required is frequent formal communication. By having a weekly or monthly written report, you are able to review what you have completed, what part you want the customer to play and most importantly, what you think needs to be done to make things go better. If you polled a group of managers, you would probably find more than 50% of them indicate that they would not want to share their problems with customers. There is a natural fear that the information will be used against you. In greater than 90% of my dealings with customers, I have found that not only will they not use that information against you; they will display an increased respect and trust in you. Sure, there is always an exception- it also a customer that you probably don't want. Stew Leonard's, a famous grocer in Connecticut that grosses more per square foot than any other grocer has a rock at their entrance. On the rock are inscribed two rules. Rule 1 says the customer is always right. Rule 2 says if the customer is wrong refer to rule 1. The message which I take away from it is that you should do everything possible to satisfy your customer. If you can't do that, they probably shouldn't or won't be your customer much longer. The written communiqué helps you tell the customer what you heard and what you will do to improve the situation. In some cases, you may even be able to tell the customer what he could do to help you both. In implementing this practice of just asking how things went or how they should go, you are differentiating your organization from your competition and setting a standard by which others will be evaluated. Some organizational experts would indicate that this is the basis for continual improvement. I would prefer to say that this is the basis for continual product renewal or evolution. In today's world, new products and services are evolving daily.

Maintaining the status quo is not adequate for survival. More importantly, maintaining the status quo will result in declining margins. As stated in the previous chapter, your business is in the business to make money. Being better than the rest, while doing so in an efficient manner, is how you make money. You cannot assume that efficiency in one area of your business is understood by all. Communicating successes not only help your team feel good, but also help them learn from others successes. This constant learning enables others to understand where they, too, can be more agile. Good communication, or sharing both successes and failures, enables your team to be more agile. They know that growth requires occasional risk, and that an occasional failure can be a learning experience for future growth, as long as it is consistent with your strategic direction.

Chapter 10

Deliver Faster and Cheaper

More Value Does Not Mean Cheaper,
Remind Them What You Are Doing

BEING THE MOST efficient will help you improve your market position for a while. If you do not have a patented or copyright process, it won't take long for your competition to either match or exceed in efficiency. Efficiency is not a marketing strategy by itself. It can help you gain a temporary competitive edge, albeit temporary. Your customers when asked will tell you that they want it cheaper and faster. Marketing experts will tell you that more value is not necessarily cheaper. Therein lays the problem.

Perception is reality

You need to find the balance between added value and less expensive. Properly perceived, you can charge more. If not perceived, it doesn't matter. The best way to create the added value is with a true ROI which your customer can sell internally. It is much easier to convince their management that they paid more for your product or services <u>and</u> they saved their company money. This is obviously an easier sell then trying to explain why they paid more. The average customer does not know what they want because they don't know what you can do to help them. Yes, they will ask for more, faster, cheaper; but they will expect you to figure it out. You can figure it out by asking them what they like, don't like, and what they need. It is your job to develop a better offering, by asking individual customers and differentiating market needs from individual needs. Only you understand what your company or you can do, the customer does not.

Your job is to identify what is custom and what is better. Everyone knows that custom costs more. In a free market, custom will generate more revenue, but in many cases that cost will be beyond the range of the average customer. You should price custom work appropriately since you don't make it up in volume. Custom work inhibits you, if you have limited resources, from addressing other customer needs. You want to therefore identify what is custom (more appropriately, what is unique) and what is efficient. When you are able to identify this combination, then you truly have the ability to deliver faster and cheaper for comparable offerings- not just the fastest and cheapest!

Communicate to know where your company is viewed

Customers should be reminded what you are doing for them. Unless you communicate on a regular basis, while this may be understood at one level in the organization, it may not be perceived at other levels. The other less frequently contacted individuals will let you know whether there is perceived value. Unfortunately, perception and reality do not always meet.

Understanding those differences are only achieved through ongoing dialog. Unless your operation is a one man show, you also need to understand how others within your organization impact the customer. For example, if you do everything possible to satisfy your customer and your billing organization continually sends out erroneous and late bills, will your customer be happy? Receiving a correct bill is a basic assumption that your customer will have. Improving on the incorrect process has no perceived incremental value. On the other hand, improving on the process of billing such that the customer receives a correct bill and the cost of preparation is less for your company enables both to perceive value. Each customer facing touch point should be assessed in this fashion. It is not prudent that you detail flowchart each touch point for each customer. You can't afford it nor do you have the resources to do so. This is where the survey results pay for themselves. If a significant number of your customers have the same issue then it may be beneficial to address that issue. In either case, losing sight of the overall vision does not enable you to complete your fundamental goal. Remember where we started- you need to be uncomfortable with where you are. Today is yesterday tomorrow.

Your competitors are not standing still

While you need to ensure that you are not in a constant state of paranoia, you need to be preparing for tomorrow today. The truly successful leader is able to balance this discomfort with the present and comfort with the vision for the future. As your organization evolves, so must your people. Continual education, continual customer interface, continuous improvement evolve into continual success. Your competitors are not standing still. Even if they are, new competitors can emerge. Some of you may be old enough to remember the first Japanese cars. They were cheap, but they were also not very reliable. At first they gained market share solely on pricing. The Japanese companies took their business seriously and quickly improved. They began to garner quality awards and today are positioned to surpass American made automobiles. Even today, the Japanese owned cars are made in the USA yet they exceed in quality. They truly believe in the faster and cheaper approach, and remain ahead by incorporating faster development cycles. They knew what they had to do, and ventured forward.

As you venture forward, you leave a legacy. That legacy is comprised of knowledgeable business people that you have developed. They are free to improve upon the foundation that has been built. That foundation helps them bravely weather the changing business environment in which they live. They are comfortable living in uncertainty- and that is why I Love Gray!

About the Author

Richard Jozwiakowski is a change agent. He has managed at multiple levels and developed a reputation as a turn-around specialist. He has been brought into troubled organization to correct their direction. Richard has managed organizations from as small as 3 people to over 1200. As a Vice-President at Pitney Bowes, he took a service organization that had a bad reputation with its customer base and was losing money to being an industry leader. Under his leadership, the service organization tripled revenue (from $34M to $100M). Improved profitability (from 0 to $27M), and increased customer satisfaction (from 26% totally satisfied to 70% totally satisfied and 94% satisfied). He was asked to take over a troubled acquisition, and within the first full quarter of managing that, the organization reported its best revenue in 12 years and most profitable quarter. Prior to joining Pitney Bowes, Richard turned around two other organizations by balancing customer satisfaction, people development and profitability. As a Marketing Manager for Picker International's service division, he developed programs which resulted in growing the revenue from $32M to $150M and the profit from $2M to $32M in less than 4 years. Richard has over 20 years Marketing Management experience.

Richard obtained a BS degree in Mathematics from Marquette University.

After achieving the rank of Captain in the Marine Corps, he returned to college to complete his MBA at the University of Wisconsin-Milwaukee.